W9-ACY-457

Duet

Dorianne Laux & Joseph Millar

Copyright © 2016 by Jacar Press

All rights reserved. No part of this book may be reproduced in any form or by any means without the prior written permission of the Publisher, excepting brief quotations used in connection with reviews.

Some of these poems have previously appeared in the magazines *APR, Brilliant Corners, Chicago Quarterly Review, Crab Orchard Review, Poet Lore, Paris-American, line/break, River Styx, Diode,* and *Fortune,* and in the collections *Overtime, Blue Rust,* and *Kingdom,* the latter three all from Carnegie Mellon University Press.

Cover & interior design: Daniel Krawiec

ISBN 978-0-936481-16-6

Jacar Press
6617 Deerview Trail
Durham, NC 27712
www.jacarpress.com

Who Do You Love

This is the night after Bo Diddley died
and we sit in the café drinking iced tea
reading his lyrics in the newspaper
along with the story of the hairline crack
in the left front hoof of Big Brown,
another American original.
Outside the long cars prowl the dusk
trailing their ribbons of smoke,
heat lightning flickers over the street
and the waitress Arlene
brings salsa and chips.

I want to say thanks
for the cavernous voice
and the black cowboy hat,
the triangle rhinestone Fender guitar
and the scratchy beat everyone stole—
Quicksilver, Willie Dixon, The Who,
easy to shuffle to,
easy to dance to:
"walk 47 miles of barb wire
with a cobra snake for a necktie"
Chonk-chicka-chicka-chonk-chonk.

Listening to Paul Simon

Such a brave generation.
We marched onto the streets
in our T-shirts and jeans, holding
the hand of the stranger next to us
with a trust I can't summon now,
our voices raised in song.
Our rooms were lit by candlelight,
wax dripping onto the table, then
onto the floor, leaving dusty
starbursts we'd pop off
with the edge of a butter knife
when it was time to move.
But before we packed and drove
into the middle of our lives
we watched the leaves outside
the window shift in the wind
and listened to Paul Simon,
his tindery voice, then fell back
into our solitude, leveled our eyes
on the American horizon
that promised us everything
and knew it was never true:
smoke and cinders, insubstantial
as fingerprints on glass.
It isn't easy to give up hope,
to escape a dream. We shed
our clothes and cut our hair,
our former beauty piled at our feet.
And still the music lived inside us,
whole worlds unmaking us in the dark,
so that sleeping and waking we heard
the train's distant whistle, steel
trestles shivering across the land
that was still ours in our bones and hearts,
its lone headlamp searching the weedy
stockyards, the damp, gray rags of fog.

Donut Shop Jukebox

Each morning Willis plays checkers
with Eddie, the meth addict 40 days clean
who says he can see the board's white fibers
running from square to square.
Inside it smells of coffee and sugar,
the Shirelles singing Baby It's You
and someone taps on the fogged up
window, late for work, needing
jumper cables. In the fields beyond
where the ditch runs with water
the star thistle opens its stunned
furry leaves, dry needles jabbing the air.

I like the engine roaring to life, a savage
red dogwood shedding its flowers
over the sidewalk, over the fence.
I like your hat with its purple feather,
cheap as a melody, cheap as a wish.

Cher

I wanted to be Cher, tall
as a glass of iced tea,
her bony shoulders draped
with a curtain of dark hair
that plunged straight down,
the cut tips brushing
her non-existent butt.
I wanted to wear a lantern
for a hat, a cabbage, a piñata
and walk in thigh high boots
with six inch heels that buttoned
up the back. I wanted her
rouged cheek bones and her
throaty panache, her voice
of gravel and clover, the hokum
of her clothes: black fishnet
and pink pom-poms, frilled
halter tops, fringed bells
and her thin strip of waist
with the bullet hole navel.
Cher standing with her skinny arm
slung around Sonny's thick neck,
posing in front of the Eiffel Tower,
The Leaning Tower of Piza,
The Great Wall of China,
The Crumbling Pyramids, smiling
for the camera with her crooked
teeth, hit-and-miss beauty, the sun
bouncing off the bump on her nose.
Give me back the old Cher,
the gangly, imperfect girl
before the shaving knife
took her, before they shoved
pillows in her tits, injected
the lumpy gel into her lips.
Take me back to the woman

I wanted to be, stalwart
and silly, smart as her lion
tamer's whip, my body a torch
stretched the length of the polished
piano, legs bent at the knee, hair
cascading down over Sonny's blunt
fingers as he pummeled the keys,
singing in a sloppy alto
the oldest, saddest songs.

Monk

Monk sat alone under the stars
dim and few as they were
incognito on a park bench
with nothing to pawn
and nothing to fence
his large fingers flexed
then halfway clenched.
He was thinking of music
the way a regular person
might be thinking of lunch.

He was thinking of Ruby
and thinking of tears,
some chords he could thumb left handed,
some mathmatical renegade harmonics,
and maybe a tall cold gin and tonic,
not to mention a melody
that would sound like running downstairs.

He could think about music anywhere
brushing his hair or tying his shoes.
Sometimes it sounded like rag time or stride
or some geological landscape —
mineral and rock, volcanic shale,
lying just under the blues —
with its minor tones
muffled deep in the earth,
its phrasings that lasted
an extra beat,
which others could study
though no one could tell
what storms raged under his hat's
pinched crown
and over the quiet shores of his heart
what polar tides rose
and fell down.

Torch Singer

I could imagine her yellow skirt
rustling like a late summer breeze
over the mesh of her nylons
walking downstage, holding the mike
against her mouth
like a piece of intimate hardware
and sighing the lyrics to Cry Me a River.

That's how I thought of Julie London
before I heard she married Jack Webb
Dragnet's favorite TV cop
who took such pride in being square
you could almost like him:
"Just tell us what happened. ma'am,
that's what we're here for."
Always faintly aloof and admonitory
in his narrow tie and brogan shoes,
always clean shaven and matter of fact.
How could she marry a guy like that?

But the streets of LA and its nightclubs
were like some dazzling, forbidden realm
far from western Pennsylvania
with its sandlot baseball and bloody nose,
its slag piles and abandoned mines.

I was trying to grow an imagination
from newsreels and cowboy movies,
not to mention the gorgeous shape
of the music teacher's ass
and the muscle cars like the Rocket 88,
somebody's uncle's pride and joy
with 18 layers of ivory baked
onto the fenders and deck lid

and Gene Vincent in his pompador
singing Woman Love from the dashboard.
And so I knew Julie was too good for him.
I watched the pale moths double in the air
and dreamed again of her husky voice,
her long legs and long auburn hair.

Lightnin' Hopkins Returns Home

The country lay below him like a woman
when he looked from the railroad trestle
carrying the worn suitcase
and watching out for snakes.
He listened to the whistle die away
beyond the fields, stepped across the fencewire
through the canebrake east of town
as though entering a church.

He sat down gazing at the feed store's porch,
the hound asleep in the Texas dust
and the sad mule standing by itself –
gathered them into the shadows
behind his dark glasses, till the blues
began to pace forth
like mourners at a funeral:
Money Taker, Mr. Charlie,
Bald Headed Woman, Shine On Moon
bowing slowly to each other
over the bridge of the old guitar.

Mick Jagger (World Tour, 2008)

He stands on stage
after spot-lit stage, yowling
with his rubber mouth. If you
turn off the sound he's
a ruminating bovine,
a baby's face tasting his first
sour orange or spitting
spooned oatmeal out.
Rugose cheeks and beef
jerky jowls, shrubby hair
waxed, roughed up, arms
slung dome-ward, twisted
branches of a tough tree, knees
stomped high as his sunken chest.
Oddities aside, he's a hybrid
of stamina and slouch,
tummy pooch, pouches under
his famous invasive rolling eyes.
He flutters like the pages
of a dirty book, doing
the sombrero dance, rocking
around the microphone's
round black foot , one hand
gripping the skinny metal rod,
the other pumping its victory fist
like he's flushing a chain toilet.
Old as the moon and sleek
as a puma circling the herd,
a slim redwood on one shaggy leg,
head in the clouds, arms full
of skinks, tree rats, black-capped
birds. The vein on his forehead

pops. His hands drop into fists.
He bows like a beggar then rises
like a monarch. Sir Mick,
our bony ruler. Jagger, slumping
off stage shining with sweat.
Oh please don't die, not now,
not ever, not yet.

Georgia on My Mind

Like a low-rent version of Frank O'Hara
I'm stranded here at the checkout stand
when I see the headline:
"Ray Charles Is Dying"

though I'm not buying French cigarettes
or cigars or a bottle of Strega,
whatever that is.

No flower stalls or Mediterranean kiosks
line the streets of this dim neighborhood,
only a twenty-four-hour Albertson's

where I wait, more alone than before
with my lunchmeat and discount cereal,
my peanuts and Diet Coke.

He looks yellow, wasted, eaten away
draped in a silver gabardine suit,
the angel of death leaning over him —

"Alien Trapped in a Kansas Silo"
on the cover of the tabloid *Globe*.

America's nightbound genius musician
who kicked heroin in '65
drinking coffee with sugar and Bols gin.

The world's greatest male jazz singer
(I'm sorry Joe Williams, who collapsed on the street
after walking away from a Vegas hotel

and Mel Torme with dimes on your eyes
in a Los Angeles funeral home...)

Angel, my hands are dirty too
but I don't want to die alone like this
with my breath of old torch songs, forgotten blues —

Lonely Avenue, Losin' Hand,
other arms reach out to me
in a hotel near the train station
watching the rain come down.

Dolly's Breasts

are singing
from the rafters of her chest,
swaying beneath sheeny satin,
suspended in the choreography
of her bra: twin albino dolphins
breaching from her ball gown's
rhinestone cleavage. Her breasts
are sisters praying at twilight, a pair
of fat-cheeked Baptists dreaming
of peaches, her nipples the color
of autumn, two lonely amber eyes.
When she shakes her metallic bodice,
tinsel swimming up her pink fonts
of nourishment, the spotlight hums
and shimmies with them, the audience,
open-mouthed, stunned into silence
as she crosses her legs and bows, her hair
hanging down, a permed curl caught
in that soft, improbable seam.

"Music My Rampart"

I can point to the exact place in my chest
where James Taylor's voice reverberates.
I have no defense against that tenor, those
minor keys. It rushes through the aisles of my body
like a priest on dope, trailing smoke, his crucifix
caught in the folds of his robe. I can know
anything I want to know, but my body reveals me.
I sink down beneath the notes, each light-cracked step.
There are nights I jerk awake as if the phone
had rung. But there's no sound except
the refrigerator humming, the joists creaking
in the cold. I watch moonlight move
across the wall and it's as if I could touch
my own sadness, the rooms flung with filaments
that loom in the pockets of my closed eyes.
There's no accounting for it. I open my mouth
and sing Sweet Baby James. I cross my hands
over my breasts like a woman who is happy to die.

Zulu, Indiana (An Ode to the Internet)

Zulu, Indiana is an unincorporated town on old U.S. 30,
named after the South African Tribe Paul Simon sang beside
on Graceland. Graceland, home of Elvis Presley,
far from Johannesburg where native Joseph Shabalala's
Ladysmith Black Mambazo gave Simon the Zulu nickname
Vulindlela - He who has opened the gate. Johannesburg,

Sister city to New York where millions of people speak
800 languages and listen to Paul Simon, as they do in Zulu,
Indiana where there is only one person with the surname Zulu,
Andrew Zulu, Zulu meaning heaven, place of endless burial,
yellow, mirror less, the opposite of Graceland, which has
mirrored stairs and ceilings, and five graves: grandmother,

mother, father, Elvis and his still-born twin. Graceland,
a one family town with one white-columned mansion
which features an indoor jungle, complete with waterfall,
although according to Albert Goldman, "Nothing in the house
is worth a dime." I like that. And that Paul Simon after seeing
Elvis perform Bridge Over Troubled Water in Vegas

(circa 1970), was reported to have said, "That's it,
we might as well all give up now." But Paul did not give up,
and went on to compose "African Skies" and Joseph Shabalala
who was born a herd boy in the township of Ladysmith has gone
on to outsell, in his country, the Beatles and Michael Jackson.
And one Andrew Zulu, who I found on Facebook, looks about 12

and loves Lil Wayne. Lil Wayne, born in New Orleans, son
of a 19 year old mother, a father who left for good two years later,
who wrote his first rap song at the age of eight and left it
on the record company's answering machine. Lil Wayne,
a man with a thousand tattoos: on his back a prayer
in cursive script, on his belly the name of a band

he once belonged to, one palm inscribed with the word gun,
a trigger finger that says *trigger*. Even his eyelids are tattooed,
the left says *fear*, the right, *god*. Lil Wayne, who before
he was ferried to Rikers on weapons charges
had 8 root canals, then paid to have 150,000 dollars worth
of diamonds embedded in his teeth. His dentist, Dr. Mongalo,

when asked about the price, quoted Don Quixote, saying
A tooth is worth more than a diamond. Diamonds, major export
of South Africa and the shimmer behind Grand Apartheid, the Sixties,
when Joseph had to have a pass to travel across his own city. By now,
many young people in Soweto don't much remember Apartheid
and have become part of the middle class called "Black Diamonds".

One Tana Sigasa, during the anti-Apartheid struggle, hid his AK-47
under his bed with his guitar, the case used to smuggle messages
and weapons between exiled South Africans in Botswana and Soweto.
Paul Simon wrote "Diamonds on the Soles of her Shoes", a song
whose triadic harmonies I can't get out of my head. Simon says
the song is a-political, even though critics swear it's hidden in the lyrics.

Sigasa has been to Soweto's Maponya Mall but says its glittering
new world has no appeal. "There were many who lined their pockets
after the victory over Apartheid. The poor were left behind."
He says he believes that the corruption charges against President Zuma,
(also referred to by his initials, JZ), who was once was arrested
for his anti-Apartheid beliefs, and is now accused of corruption,

racketeering, fraud and rape, is the work of malicious conspirators.
"Zuma's blood flows with the people," Sigasa says, and points
to the words in red on the back of his T-shirt: "The Struggle Continues."
I could not find the reason behind the naming of the town of Zulu,
and until this morning did not know that unincorporated means
a place outside the municipal council, remote areas

with low populations, the territory not formally incorporated
into the United States and therefore subject to being sold
or transferred to another power, or, conversely, being granted
independence. In other words, little kingdoms
within the kingdom, with their own ceremonies
and frictions, their own ears of corn and antelope horns,

their homegrown wines of basement vintage.
Whatever we are afraid of, it will change. Whatever
mistakes we make, we will become what we are
because of our blunders. These are the syllables
I sing as I rummage through my purse at the end
of a long day, looking for something, then forgetting

what it is: *Tan na na, ta na na na na.*

Dorianne Laux's most recent collections are *The Book of Men*, winner of the Paterson Poetry Prize and *Facts about the Moon*, winner of the Oregon Book Award. Laux is also author of *Awake, What We Carry*, and *Smoke* from BOA Editions. She teaches poetry in the MFA Program at North Carolina State University.

Joseph Millar is the author of *Kingdom, Blue Rust, Fortune*, and *Overtime*, which was a finalist for the Oregon Book Award. He has received grants from the National Endowment for the Arts and the Guggenheim Foundation. He teaches at Pacific University's Low Residency MFA Program.